GROWING UP
UNDER A RED FLAG

A MEMOIR OF SURVIVING THE CHINESE CULTURAL REVOLUTION

WRITTEN BY **YING CHANG COMPESTINE**

ILLUSTRATED BY **XINMEI LIU**

ROCKY POND BOOKS

In memory of Dr. Chang Sin Liu—I love you, Daddy! —Y.C.C.

ROCKY POND BOOKS
An imprint of Penguin Random House LLC, New York

First published in the United States of America by Rocky Pond Books, an imprint of Penguin Random House LLC, 2024
Text copyright © 2024 by Ying Chang Compestine
Illustrations copyright © 2024 by Xinmei Liu

Visit us online at PenguinRandomHouse.com.

Library of Congress Cataloging-in-Publication Data is available. • ISBN 9780593533987 • 10 9 8 7 6 5 4 3 2 1

Manufactured in Italy

LEG • Design by Sylvia Bi • Text set in Aldus Nova Pro • The art was created with ink using dip pens and colored digitally.

This is a work of nonfiction. Some names and identifying details have been changed.

The publisher does not have any control over and does not assume any responsibility for author or third-party websites or their content.

I was born in Wuhan, China. In 1966, when I was three years old, the leader of China, Mao Zedong, declared a Cultural Revolution to get rid of his opponents and to regain his power over the government. He punished educated people like my parents, who disagreed with him.

My parents worked as doctors. My father was a surgeon
and my mother was a traditional Chinese doctor who
treated patients with herbs and acupuncture needles.
We lived in the hospital compound.

The nights when Father didn't have to perform surgeries, he taught me English and told me stories about San Francisco, where his American teacher, Dr. Smith, lived. Dr. Smith had to leave Wuhan after the Communists took over China. He gave Father a picture of the Golden Gate Bridge and invited him to work with him in his hometown of San Francisco. But Father didn't want to leave his patients.

I dreamt of going to America and eating foods with funny names like hot dogs, pizza, Twinkies, tater tots, and banana splits.

My mother wasn't always pleased with me because I didn't behave like a traditional Chinese girl—speaking in a low voice, playing piano, and learning the fan dance. But my father loved my curiosity and strong spirit. He answered my endless questions and clapped with me when I sang English folk songs at the top of my lungs.

The year I turned five, we were no longer allowed to read English books or speak in foreign languages. But Father and I secretly continued our English lessons. He told me, "Remember, my dear, knowledge is power. One day you will have a chance to use it." I wasn't sure when and where I would ever be allowed to speak English outside of our home.

Everyone was busy with revolutionary activities,
so there were not enough people to work in the
factories. When our building's electricity went out,
we would close the curtains and light a small candle.
The high point of those days was hiding under a
blanket and listening to songs from the American
international broadcast *Voice of America*.

Our life soon changed for the worse. Mao's portraits and teachings hung on walls all over the city. We were ordered to wear Mao uniforms, Mao buttons, and to carry *The Little Red Book,* which contained Mao's teachings. I was sad I could no longer wear my chrysanthemum flower dress.

Food and other daily necessities became scarce. We were issued ration tickets. Red was for eggs, green for meat, and yellow for soap. But the shelves at the store were always empty.

One day, Comrade Li moved into Father's study. At first, I thought he was my friend because he folded origami birds and used them to trade food with me. But soon, I understood why my parents were afraid of him.

Comrade Li was the leader of the Red Guard, an organization made up of teenage students. The group claimed they were Mao's most loyal followers. They marched around the neighborhood, singing revolutionary songs and dragging away anyone who didn't conform, like our friends who lived upstairs, Dr. Wong and Mrs. Wong. They destroyed items that were considered Western, like sewing machines, refrigerators, and space heaters.

I sensed danger was near when Father came home with a letter from Dr. Smith. He whispered to Mother, "Someone opened the letter. We can't write to him anymore."

The next day, Father walked me home from school. When we got to the courtyard, the air smelled of ink. Our building was covered in posters. Comrade Li drew a red X as bright as blood over Father's name on one of the posters. The Red Guards were stomping on the flowers in our garden while their speakers blared out revolutionary songs.

"Why are they doing this, Daddy?" I whispered. Father didn't answer; he only held my hand tighter.

Once in our apartment, he ran to the fireplace, lit a fire, and burned stacks of letters and books. Wisps of ash bumped around the fireplace like frightened butterflies. Father even threw in the English lesson book we had made together.

I watched the fire slowly destroy the picture
of the happy girl on the cover—first her hair,
then her face, and finally her ice cream and
dress. Tears rolled down my face. My happy
days were burning along with her.

I held my breath when Father picked up the picture of the Golden
Gate Bridge in San Francisco. How I wished I could go there now.
Father stared at it intently and mumbled, "I can't do it. Not yet."

"Daddy, you can hide it there!" I pointed at the picture
frame that held Mao's portrait.

Suddenly we heard doors banging, dishes breaking,
and people screaming from upstairs.

Mother rushed in.
"They are coming!" she cried.

Our door was kicked open. Comrade Li stormed inside with a group of Red Guards. They tore our silk comforters, smashed our radio, grabbed mother's pearl necklace from her dresser and slammed it against the wall. Mother wept and I clenched Father's arm, trembling.

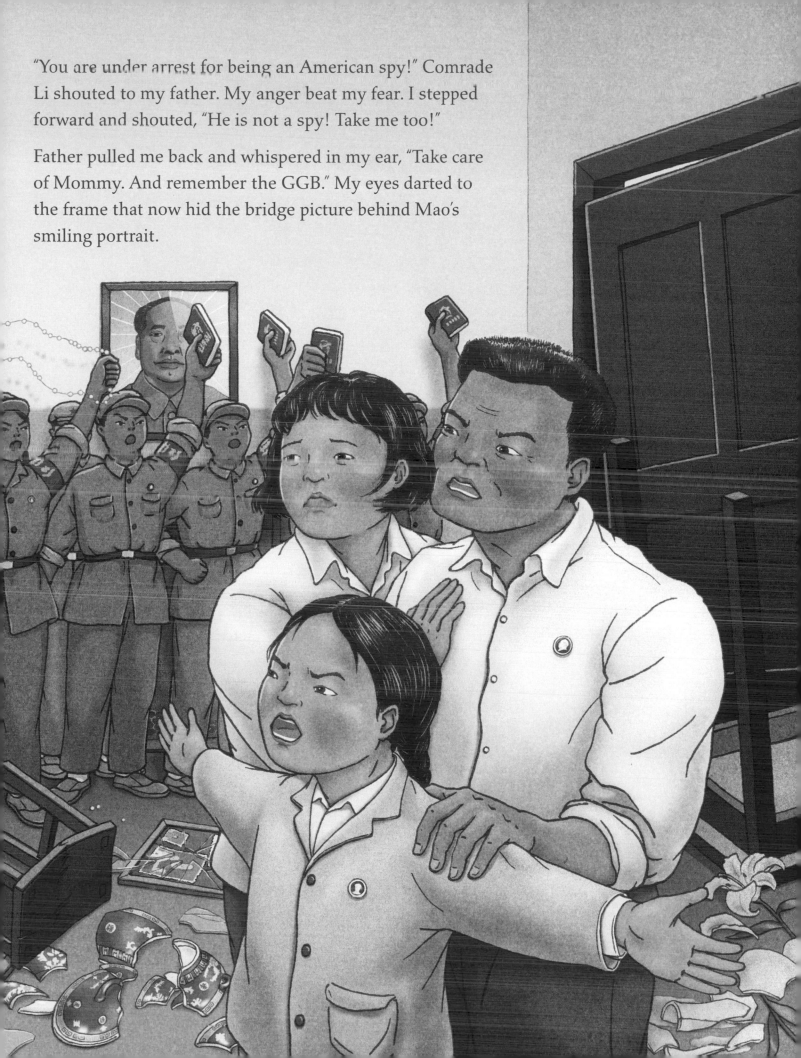

"You are under arrest for being an American spy!" Comrade Li shouted to my father. My anger beat my fear. I stepped forward and shouted, "He is not a spy! Take me too!"

Father pulled me back and whispered in my ear, "Take care of Mommy. And remember the GGB." My eyes darted to the frame that now hid the bridge picture behind Mao's smiling portrait.

The days seemed so much longer without Father. I wrapped myself in his scarf and practiced English words. At night, I longed for his comfort when I awoke from nightmares. I missed him even more when I looked at the picture of the Golden Gate Bridge. I dreamt that one day we could go there together and eat food with funny names.

Mother became quiet and sad. She had to work
all the time, so I took on the duty of buying food.

One day when I was eight years old, Mother woke me up and
said, "Hurry! A patient just told me they are going to have meat
and soap today at the market. I must go back to work now."
Half-asleep, I rushed down the dark, cold street.

A big crowd was already gathering outside the market. I took out the ration tickets and pushed myself through the horde of people.

Someone stepped on my shoe and it came off. When I bent over to pick it up, a big boy snatched my tickets and ran. One shoe in hand, I chased him for two long blocks. When I caught up to him, I stomped and yelled and hit him with my shoe until he gave me back my ration tickets.

I fought my way back to the store entrance and bought the meat, but there was no soap in sight. When I told Mother how I got the food, she gave me a rare hug and said, "You have grown up, my dear."

Life became even harder when summer came. The city was as hot as a burning stove. One day, I came home from the market longing to take a bath to wash off the dirt and sweat, but the water to our building had been shut off and we had run out of soap weeks ago.

Mother took the basket full of sandy vegetables from me and gasped.

"Oh, dear, what's in your hair?!" She moved closer to me and said, "Lice! Yes, it's lice." She sat me down, emptied the last bit of coal oil from our lamp, and dipped her ox-bone comb into it to kill the lice.

But my hair was too thick to be combed. She retrieved a pair of scissors and Father's razor and said, "We have to shave your head."

I jumped out of the chair and cried,
"No! There must be another way."

Tears welled up in Mother's eyes. "I don't know
what else to do, Ying. If I don't shave your hair,
the lice will spread throughout the apartment."

Watching Mother cry hurt me more
than the thought of losing my hair.
I closed my eyes and said,
"Fine! Do what you must!"

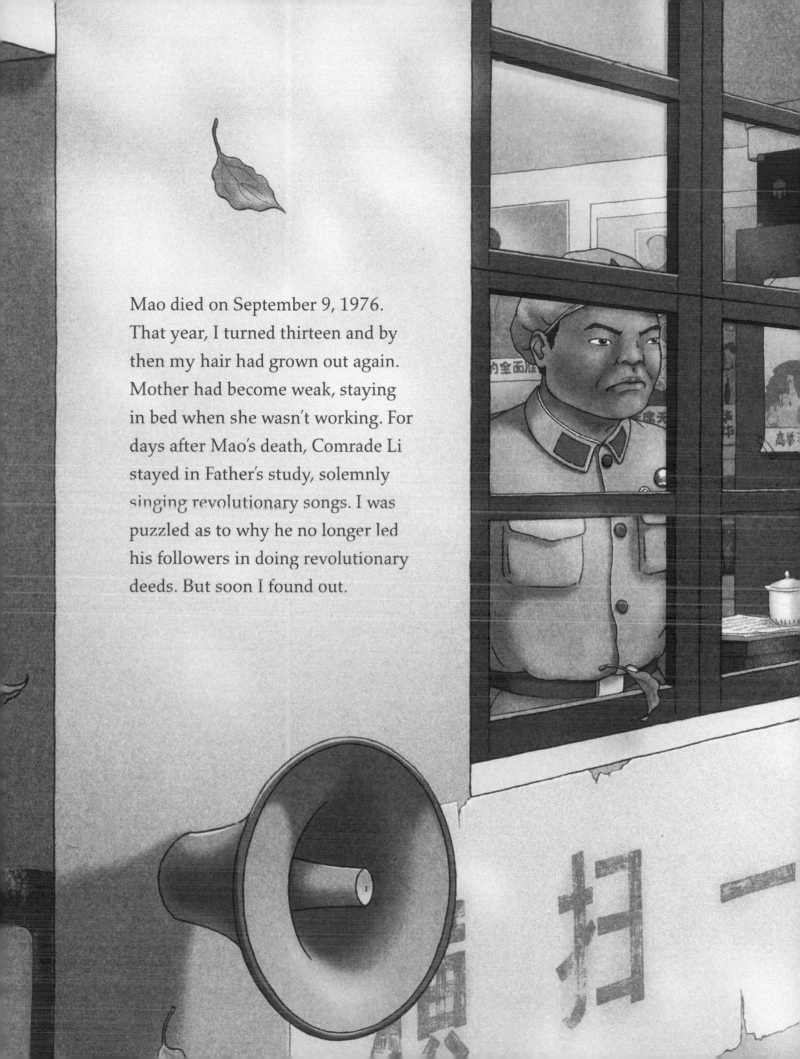

Mao died on September 9, 1976. That year, I turned thirteen and by then my hair had grown out again. Mother had become weak, staying in bed when she wasn't working. For days after Mao's death, Comrade Li stayed in Father's study, solemnly singing revolutionary songs. I was puzzled as to why he no longer led his followers in doing revolutionary deeds. But soon I found out.

One sunny day the next month, a car raced into the courtyard. Two soldiers jumped out and marched toward our apartment. My heart jumped in my chest. I looked at my frail mother, and my heart rate quickened. How would I stop them from taking Mother away?

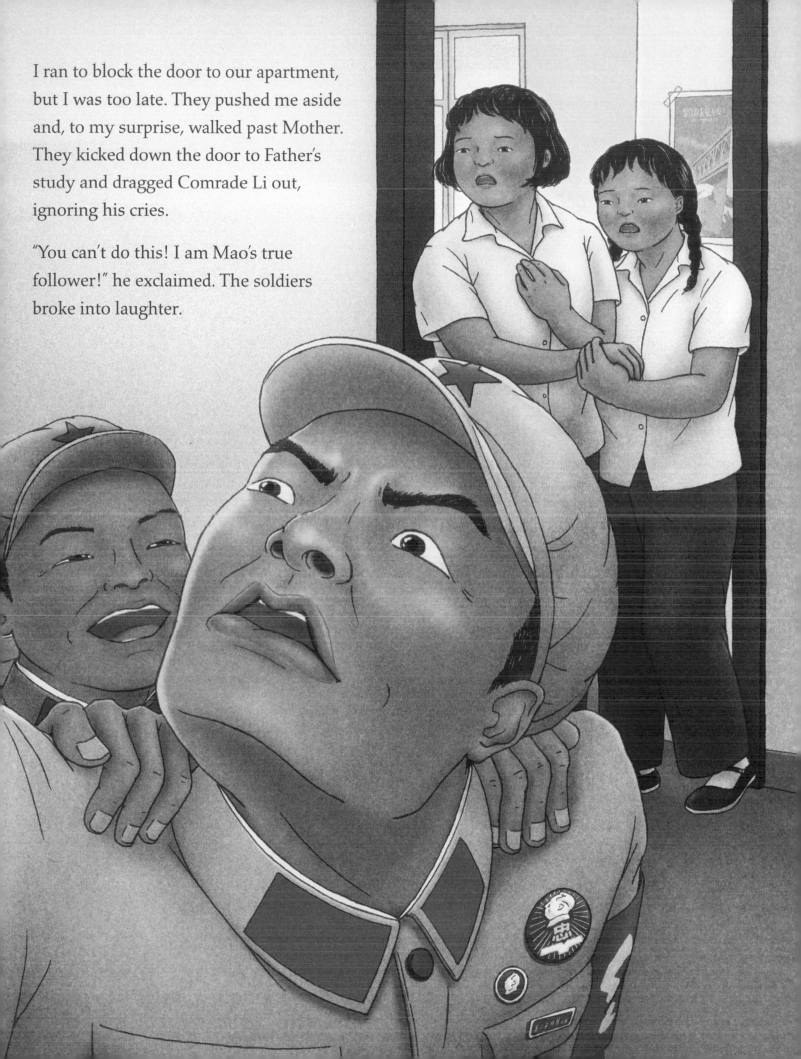

I ran to block the door to our apartment, but I was too late. They pushed me aside and, to my surprise, walked past Mother. They kicked down the door to Father's study and dragged Comrade Li out, ignoring his cries.

"You can't do this! I am Mao's true follower!" he exclaimed. The soldiers broke into laughter.

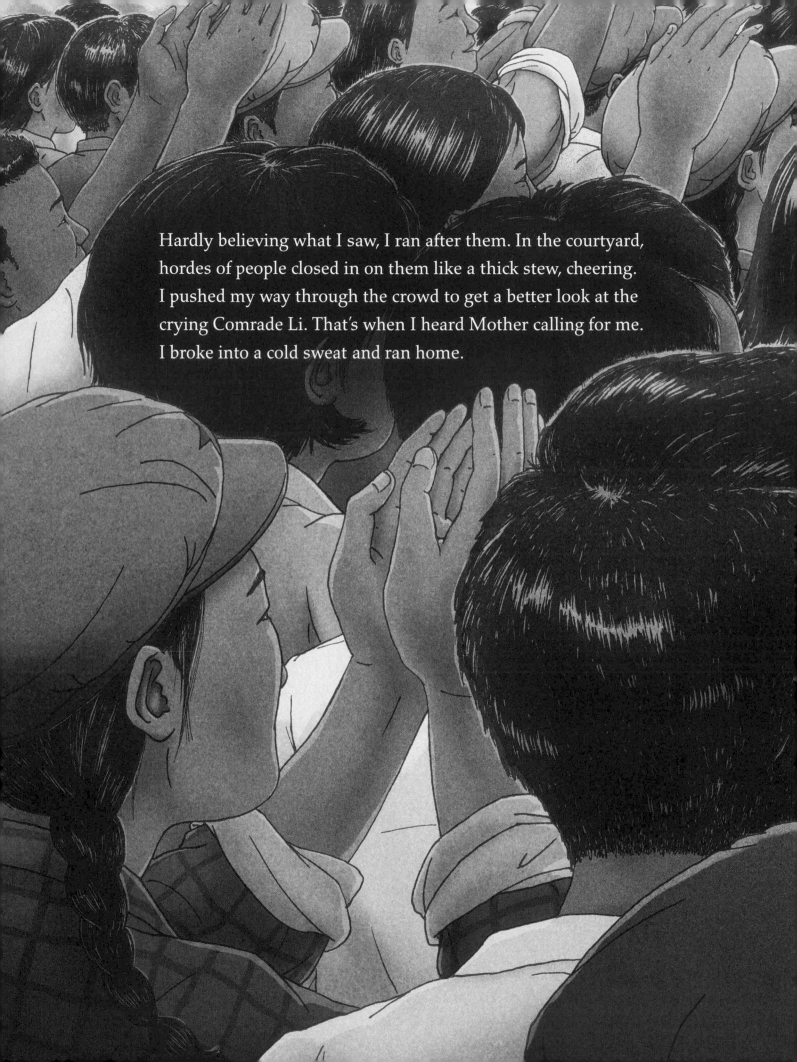

Hardly believing what I saw, I ran after them. In the courtyard, hordes of people closed in on them like a thick stew, cheering. I pushed my way through the crowd to get a better look at the crying Comrade Li. That's when I heard Mother calling for me. I broke into a cold sweat and ran home.

Someone flung open our door. It was Father! I had dreamt of this moment, practicing a thousand times what I would say. Now all I could do was stare.

Father opened his arms. "Come here, my beautiful girl!" Mother joined us. Father wrapped his arms around us tightly. We stood there for a long time until I asked, "Daddy, how did you get out?"

"They had to let me go to make room for people like Comrade Li," said Father. His laughter echoed the firecrackers in the distance, cheering the arrest of Mao's wife and her political group, the "Gang of Four," and celebrating the true end of the Cultural Revolution.

Two months before my twenty-third birthday,
I left China to study in America. The following
Chinese New Year, my parents came to visit.
Dr. Smith held a dinner party for us at his home,
overlooking the Golden Gate Bridge. He served
all the foods with funny names: hot dogs, pizza,
Twinkies, and banana splits.

迎春

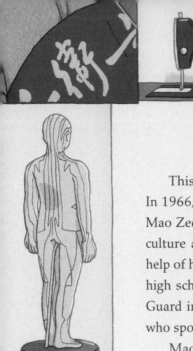

AUTHOR'S NOTE

This is the story of my childhood growing up during the Chinese Cultural Revolution. In 1966, the ensuing power struggle among the Communist leaders resulted in Chairman Mao Zedong launching the Cultural Revolution. He wanted to destroy traditional Chinese culture and anything considered Western to regain power from his opponents. With the help of his wife, Jiang Qing, Mao organized the Red Guard, composed of middle school and high school students. Led by Mao's followers from the People's Liberation Army, the Red Guard imprisoned and murdered millions of intellectuals, opposition leaders, and anyone who spoke against Mao's ideology.

Mao's power reached its peak during the middle of the Cultural Revolution. During those years, everyone in China had to carry Mao's *Little Red Book* and wear Mao-style clothes. Radios and loudspeakers broadcast his teachings along with revolutionary songs. Every home and public space was decorated with Mao statues and quotations. China's economy reeled. Stores were empty and goods rationed.

While the Cultural Revolution officially ended in 1969, the politically charged atmosphere continued until Mao's death on September 9, 1976. On October 6, less than a month later, the new chairman of the Chinese Communist Party, Hua Guofeng, ordered the arrest of Mao's wife and her conspirators, the so-called Gang of Four.

In 1977, the universities opened after being closed for ten years. I passed the difficult university exam in 1980 and graduated in 1984. With the help of my father's American teacher, my dream finally came true: I came to the U.S. to pursue a graduate degree. The first time I saw the Golden Gate Bridge, I thought it was even more beautiful than the picture I knew so well.

I received my graduate degree from University of Colorado in Boulder in 1990. Eventually I moved to California with my husband and son. We now live near San Francisco.